Aunt
DOLLIE'S
Remedies and Tips
175 Years of Home
REMEDIES

Aunt DOLLIE'S Remedies and Tips
175 Years of Home REMEDIES

CLEMENTINE HOLMES BASS

iUniverse LLC
Bloomington

AUNT DOLLIE'S REMEDIES AND TIPS
175 Years of Home Remedies

iUniverse books may be ordered through booksellers or by contacting:

iUniverse LLC
1663 Liberty Drive
Bloomington, IN 47403
www.iuniverse.com
1-800-Authors (1-800-288-4677)

ISBN: 978-1-4917-0214-7 (sc)
ISBN: 978-1-4917-0216-1 (hc)
ISBN: 978-1-4917-0215-4 (ebk)

Library of Congress Control Number: 2013914675

Printed in the United States of America

iUniverse rev. date: 09/10/2013

Contents

Preface xi

The Early Years 1

Taking Care of the Teeth 5

    Sip Arthritis Away 8

    Pick-Me-Upper 8

    Liniment for Arthritis 8

Taking Care of Babies and Children 10

    Old-Time Fable, but It Works!..11

    Tiny Babies 11

    Diaper Rash 12

    Bed-Wetting 12

    Teething 12

    Century-Old Cure for Fever 12

    Curing Colic 13

    Head Lice and Red Bugs (Chiggers) 13

Tapeworms 14

175 Years of Home Remedies..17

    Pellagra 19

    Asthma 20

    Coughs 20

    Coughs and Sore Throats 21

    Croup 21

    Laryngitis 22

    Tonsillitis 22

    Colds and Congestion 22

    Sore Throat 22

    Diverticulitis 23

    Bleeding 24

    The Eyes 24

Earache 25
Stomach Spasms 25
Hiccups 25
Scalp 26
Boils 26
Warts 26
Headache 27
Fish Bone Stuck in the Throat 27
Heartburn 28
Monthly Period Pain 28
Sunburn 28
Nosebleed 28
Leg Ache 29
Chapped Skin 29
Upset Stomach 29
Diarrhea 29
Measles 30
Bruises 30
Insect Stings 30
Swelling and Sprain 30
Bronchitis 30
Springtime Tonic 31
Pains 31
Lullaby Pill 31
Itch 31
Sores 31
Painkiller..32
Sores, Boils, Carbuncle, and Staph Infection 32
Sore with Fever and Infection 32
Bee Sting or Stepping on a Rusted Nail 32
Snake Bites 33
Moles That Bear Watching 33
Brown Spots on Hands and Face 33
To Harden Soft Nails 34
Foot Perspiration and Odor 34

One-Step Home Remedies 35
Century-Old Household and Garden Tips 37
Planting Time 47
In the Kitchen 50
Wash Day 51
Household Aids 53
Author Not 63

This book is dedicated to the second generation
of Ed and Rosie Holmes.

Preface

My father would drive down an old, rocky road and then down a trail surrounded by trees and thickets to a gate in an old wooden fence. Beyond the fence was the small white house where Aunt Dollie lived. Aunt Dollie always seemed to be happy; she always had a dip of snuff and a wide grin. I loved listening to her talk. Her house always had an aroma of something in the oven—baked sweet potatoes, cornbread, cookies, or a cake. I recall being congested with a very bad cold. Aunt Dollie had the cure: cow chip tea. Following her directions, my mother started to boil the ingredients. The aroma was so pungent it made me sick, so I went to bed and pretended to be asleep. Nevertheless, I was soon called to the kitchen and instructed to drink the concoction. I cried, but it did not matter. Aunt Dollie told me to hold my nose and drink, so I did. I must say that I felt better almost immediately. This was one of many times Aunt Dollie cured my ills. She said that it did not make sense to buy something when she knew a remedy she could make herself. After finishing high school, I attended the University of Arkansas at Pine Bluff, which was thirty miles from Rison, where Aunt Dollie lived. I relied on Aunt Dollie to help my college friends and me with our ailments, which was invaluable to us. After college, I received a master's degree and an administrative certification. I taught kindergarten for sixteen years prior to assuming the duties of a public school administrator for fifteen years. Aunt Dollie was so proud of my accomplishments, and she often offered advice, which she called common sense, during my tenure in education. She passed away at eighty-five years of age; however, her remedies, advice, and love are still alive.

The Early Years

I never missed an opportunity to go to Aunt Dollie's house, knowing there would be something good to eat and an unbelievable story to hear. A dirt road off the old highway in Cleveland County, Arkansas, led to my father's family's modest white framed house nestled in the woods. A lazy, sleeping dog would be resting in the yard. Every time my father said, "I'm going down to the house," I would stop what I was doing and ask to go with him. My fraternal ancestors were Choctaw Indians, and they had lived on the land. Aunt Dollie recalled that my great-grandmother lived in something like a wigwam in the woods. My grandmother would visit her mother with her children in tow, all of whom were afraid of their grandmother. She said she was a really small woman with long, white braids And her eyes were like two black holes in her head. She specifically remembered hiding behind my grandmother's apron so she could not see her.

The house was Aunt Dollie's. When she was eighteen, she walked to the Cleveland County, Arkansas, courthouse with Grandmother Rosa to acquire the house and land through the Homestead Act. She had the house renovated and stayed there with my grandmother until she passed away. Each summer, my aunts, uncles, and cousins would gather at the house for a family reunion. We had all sorts of things to eat and drink, and the adults drank homemade beer Aunt Dollie brewed from brown syrup and water. There was music, ball games, and talent shows, and if we were nice, we could ride Dolly the horse. The entertainment never seemed to end.

I could talk to Aunt Dollie about anything—no subject was off limits. The tradition of my ancestors was the only way my grandmother and grandfather knew to provide for the family. Grandmother did most of the farming—harvesting crops of corn, beans, squash, and greens—while Grandfather and the older boys would hunt for deer, turkey, wild hogs, and other small game. They would also fish in rivers and stop along the way offering the neighbors some of their catch. They grew their own food, cured their meat, and canned fruit and vegetables. The family had chores that required tending the garden and walking the fields.

At four o'clock each day, they had breakfast. After breakfast, each person had his or her own chores to complete. One had to feed the farm animals, and another plowed and chopped the grass. A third harvested ripe vegetables, put them in a tub, and took them to the porch. To not waste time while picking and choosing ripe fruit, the boys would shake the trees and the girls would gather the fruit from the ground. The three boys cleaned and cared for the yard, and the three girls cleaned the house, which included scrubbing the floors and making the beds.

Grandmother and all of the children worked in the yard. The chores were finished by noon, and that is when the girls would go in and cook supper and the boys would hunt or fish. When evening came, they were allowed to play prior to cleaning themselves and going to bed. They would chase, play hide-and-seek, feed and play with the dog, and run barefoot all around the eighty acres.

When I saw Aunt Dollie's feet for the first time, I could not imagine what the knots and circles were. When she noticed my blank stare, she snickered and said, "These old feet have been through some hard times." She began to tell a story about every toe and the toenail on her big toes. In Aunt Dollie's day, it was pertinent for people to take care of their feet because everyone walked everywhere they went.

I was curious as to how their feet stayed unharmed through all this. What did they do when their feet hurt or when they stubbed their toes? Aunt Dollie said that this was not of immediate concern, so they would play until something serious happened to their feet.

Aunt Dollie recalled what my grandmother would do. If their feet were sore, she would mix one cup of fresh marigold petals with a four-ounce jar of petroleum jelly in a pan over low heat for thirty minutes. This mixture would be strained through a cheesecloth. It would be stored in a jar and applied nightly as needed. The feet were to be covered with soft white cloth to protect the sheets.

Aunt Dollie also suggested buying a cake of Octagon Soap. Put the soap in a pan of warm water and soak your feet twice a day, especially at night before retiring. The soapy water would ease the pain and soften the feet.

You could also soak feet in hot, soapy water every night, using Octagon Soap by putting the cake of soap in the water. When you take your feet out, dry them off. Take some of the soft soap and rub it on corns and calluses. After about three weeks of following this procedure, your feet will be well.

For injured toes, she suggested dabbing some coal oil on a clean, white cloth, wrapping the injured toes, and tying it with a string. Change the dressing, and repeat until the toes are healed.

For deep cuts and wounds, cut a white potato in half, place it on the sore, wrap the potato around the area with a white cloth, and tie it on the wound. The next morning, remove the potato and clean the wound.

The first time I heard the phrase "I have a corn on my toe," I imagined a small, oblong blob with kernels. I soon learned that corns are annoying, sometimes painful thickenings that form on the skin of the toe. They appear to have a dry, waxy, or translucent appearance and the callus on top spreads over the flattened area of skin. Aunt Dollie said some people picked corns out of their toes with a needle that was burned on the end. I could not imagine sticking your toe with a needle. I had to know whether there was another procedure to remedy this problem. We queried area senior citizens and learned of the following remedies:

- Crush several aspirins and add homemade lard to make a paste. Spread on the corn as a salve.
- Apply castor oil on corns for several nights. The corns should soften and disappear.
- Soak a piece of lamb's wool in hot, melted lard and wrap snuggly around and under the sore toe for several days without washing it.
- Press a small wad of cotton under the corner of the toenail and leave for several days.
- Soak your feet in warm water with a cake of Octagon Soap (soap in water). When you take your feet out, dry off and take the soft soap off the cake. Rub on bunions. Do this every night for about three weeks.

Tight shoes rubbing on the toes caused the corn problem. Aunt Dollie used castor oil on her corns and calluses. Because changes of shoes were rare and far between, this problem persisted for long periods of time. Walking with bare feet was a means of avoiding this problem. She recalled dressing her father's and brother's feet when they pulled their boots off.

Taking Care of the Teeth

Unpleasant breath, cavities, and missing teeth were not at all uncommon. I would tell Aunt Dollie about teachers, church members, and neighbors who had these problems. I could not stand being around these people, and I would try to avoid them. I would tell her how their breath made me sick, but her suggestion was to hold my breath and to not disrespect them. She reminded me that they would do better if they could.

Aunt Dollie always smiled and joked about a few experiences of her own. I was not demeaning or disrespectful to these people—I would grin and bear the situation. I took my sons to visit the Easter Bunny once, and my then four-year-old son would not sit still on the bunny's lap. I went to calm him, thinking he feared the fat, furry bunny. He reached for me and said, "Mommy, the Easter Bunny's breath stinks!" Embarrassed, I removed him from the bunny's lap and tried to shush him. As I was leaving the platform, the Easter Bunny said, "I apologize. I have been working nonstop, and I guess I need a breath mint." I mumbled something, hurriedly grabbed my other son's hand, and rushed from the area.

When I told Aunt Dollie about the incident, we had a hearty laugh. She reminded me that I had behaved the very same way as a child. She said I would not answer questions of adults; instead, I would walk away and say, "Hmmm, their breath stinks." However, they would not hear my comment. That is when I asked her to tell me how people cared for their teeth and breath when they did not have toothbrushes, toothpaste, or mouthwash. I had been told that President George Washington had wooden teeth, but I later learned that was a myth. I was curious, so I asked Aunt Dollie how she had conversations with her boyfriend and kissed him when he had bad breath. She knew about remedies she had learned from her grandmother, mother, and other relatives. I was temporarily speechless when she told me if they really liked each other, they would chew fresh green pine straw. The green pine straw would clean the teeth and make the breath fresh. If they kissed, it was a simple smack on the lips.

It seemed as if older people had stronger teeth during this time. Caring for the teeth was not of high priority until there was a problem. There was a smokehouse behind Aunt Dollie's house. I remember seeing meat hanging from the ceiling and a bucket of wood smoking in the middle of the room. This was a means of curing and preserving the meat. The distinct aroma was different from anything else I had ever smelled, and if I got too close, the smoke would burn my eyes. When the meat was ready, they would bring it in for meals. The meat would remain in the smoke house during the winter. When summer came they ate vegetables and the meat left from winter. My grandfather and the boys would assure the animals were fed and fatten for slaughter in the winter.

The meat was not always moist, and their teeth had to be strong to chew the meat. Gnawing was a way to eat the meat if one had missing or bad teeth. I understood "gnawing" as sucking and holding the meat in one's mouth until it softened enough to grind it up and eat it. Aunt Dollie's family did not know anything about dentists. If a tooth were loose or painful, someone would tie a strong string around the tooth and pull it out if they could not pull it out with their fingers.

Tooth remedies were as follows:

- Toothache: Put paregoric on a cotton ball, place on the tooth, and press down. You could also take red oak tree bark from the south side of the tree, boil it, and add a pinch of salt. Hold this in your mouth until the tooth stops aching.

- Tartar: Drink a glass of water with one teaspoon apple cider vinegar during mealtime.
- Gum conditioner: Mix two teaspoons salt (not iodized) with one teaspoon of baking soda in a container and cover. Brush teeth with this mixture three to four times a week.
- White, polished teeth: Chew wood from a black gum tree and then get soot from the back of the chimney. Place and rub gums and teeth with the soot for white polished teeth. Baking soda will also work.
- Dentures: Keep strong baking soda water in a container. Place dentures in the container and cover with a lid. Your dentures will smell fresh and sweet.

One misperception is that arthritis affects people only at an older age. However, "Arthur" can visit the old and young alike. Aunt Dollie could not recall older people complaining about arthritis when she was growing up. Every member of the family had to start the morning by working. Each morning, my grandmother would get up before the children and start a fire if it were cold or open the doors and windows if it were hot. She would get warm water in the wash pan, wash her face, and start breakfast. When breakfast was almost ready, she would wake the children, who would then wash up and eat a hearty breakfast.

Aunt Dollie did not complain. She would say, "Ain't that ugly?" when something went wrong with her joints, and she wobbled.

If I decided to complain, she would stop me in the middle of the sentence and say, "You are speaking something into being. Be thankful that everything is as well as it is." According to her, young people were not made of tough stuff. She would say,

"Just keep living, and you will understand and know what I am talking about." Aunt Dollie would not let "Arthur" get her down.

This 1838 concoction would prevent a doctor's visit every time! Boil two tablespoons of castor oil; pour in a glass of orange juice. Take before breakfast. Wait three weeks and repeat, and then wait three more weeks and repeat. The doctor promised that anyone who took this at least three times a year would not have arthritis.

Here are several other remedies.

Sip Arthritis Away

One pint apple cider vinegar
One pint raw honey

Mix the ingredients well in water and place in a covered jar. Take two tablespoons three times a day or sip three times a day with meals.

Pick-Me-Upper

One tablespoon powdered sugar
One egg
Dash of salt
One tablespoon brandy

Separate the egg. Beat yolk until thick and lemon colored. Add the sugar and brandy and beat well. Beat the egg white to a stiff froth and add it. You may add one cup of milk with a little more sugar to give the mixture added strength.

Liniment for Arthritis

One ounce wintergreen oil
One ounce eucalyptus oil
One ounce camphorate oil
Half an ounce pure spirits of turpentine

Mix ingredients well. Shake well before applying.

Arthritis is not always caused by age. The repeated wear and tear of the body's joints invites arthritis. Depending on the type, arthritis may be caused by cartilage wearing down, lack of fluid, autoimmune deficiency, infection, or a combination of factors.

To avoid arthritis, Aunt Dollie kept her body active by walking, picking vegetables and fruit, cleaning, and canning.

Taking Care of Babies and Children

Aunt Dollie married four times. She said her second marriage was a result of friends daring her to marry a very ugly man. She was beautiful, intelligent, and intimidating to men, but she consented to marry him. Everyone at the wedding had a hilarious time, including the bridegroom. She went to his house, spent the night, and walked away the next morning. She found her friends and told them she wanted to help the man feel good about himself at least once in his life. She reminded them to never dare her. She did not have children.

During her third marriage, she had a miscarriage. This was extremely distressing to her, so she never tried to have children again. She adopted one of my cousins and called all of her nieces and nephews her children. I married and became pregnant after a year. Aunt Dollie gave me her collections of homemade remedies for babies. She did not like over-the-counter or prescribed medication for pregnant women.

One evening I decided to spend the night. I slept with her in her soft, cozy bed. I was so relaxed and enjoying my deep sleep when I awoke to the smell of a good country breakfast. I immediately rose from the bed and peeked in on Aunt Dollie as she stood over the stove stirring and humming. You did not come into her kitchen without washing your face and hands. I said "good morning," and washed up for breakfast.

As always, she had made homemade biscuits and cooked rice and scrambled eggs. We had plum jelly, butter and something she had fried that looked like sausage balls. We sat down to eat, said grace, and began to fill our plates. I asked her about the round fried sausage and told her how tasty it looked. She was jolly and excited when she told me, "That is squirrel brains!" You were not allowed to waste food, so I tried not to show my shock. She went on to tell me that she prepared the brains especially for me because they would make my baby intelligent.

I began to eat the biscuit and jelly. She said, "Try eating the brains. Not only are they good for the baby, but they also taste good." I reluctantly put the brain to the side of my mouth, immediately took the napkin, pretended to wipe my mouth, and slipped the brain in the napkin. I pretended to chew and squealed with delight at how delicious the brain was. She threw them in her mouth and told me to eat some more. My napkin with the discarded brains was in my left hand, and I could not wait until the dish was empty. After breakfast, I wrapped the brains with more napkins and placed the bundle in my tote bag to throw away on my way home.

Here are several remedies for babies.

Old-Time Fable, but It Works!

Babies stretch and grunt. The older they get, the worse they become. The baby cannot rest, and neither can anyone else! To cure this, when your husband pulls off his coat, wrap the child in it and let the baby sleep in it. May it be day or night, after bathing and dressing the baby don't forget to grab your husband's coat, and . . . what a relief.

Tiny Babies

This has been tried on many tiny babies. It has been found that when they cannot keep their milk, their stomachs are lacking in acid. Give a tiny spoon of baby applesauce to even the smallest infants before the bottle. You can get drops from the doctor for this, but many babies have been cured with the applesauce when the doctor could not find what was wrong. One baby went to the hospital, and there was still no cure. The home remedy—applesauce—cured it.

Diaper Rash

Use cornstarch on the baby.

Bed-Wetting

At bedtime, give the child a teaspoonful of honey. This will help in two ways. The honey will be a sedative to the nervous system, and it will attract and hold fluid during the night. You can also kill and skin a big barn rat as you would a squirrel. Cut it up and flour and season it as you would a chicken. Feed it to the bed wetter. He or she will never wet the bed again!

Teething

Kill a mole, cut off one of its feet, tie a string around the foot, and then tie the string around the baby's neck as a necklace. The teeth will pop through the gums without pain.

Century-Old Cure for Fever

Make a tea of catnip leaves. Add a few drops of paregoric and a little sugar. Give this warm tea to the baby. It is real soothing and off to sleep they go. Some adults also enjoy it. Strong black cat-nip tea with a few grains of sugar can also reduce fever.

Curing Colic

Colic is a condition in an otherwise healthy baby in which the baby shows periods of intense, unexplained fussing/crying that can last more than three hours a day for more than three days a week for more than three weeks. However, many doctors consider that definition—first described by Morris Wessel—to be overly narrow. Doctors would consider babies with sudden severe unexplained crying lasting less than three hours a day as having colic (so-called non-Wessel's colic) in reality; doctors agree that this extreme version of colic is more likely to be the final stage of a condition that has worsened for a few weeks. To help soothe colic, use the catnip tea.

Head Lice and Red Bugs (Chiggers)

Head lice are considered little bloodsuckers. The stubborn pests can burn and cause the scalp to itch. They are small and leave big bites on the skin of your head. They are contagious. They do not cause bodily harm, and they are not dangerous.

Head lice attach their eggs to the base of the hair shaft. Head lice move by crawling; they cannot hop or fly. Head-lice infestation, or pediculosis, is spread most commonly by close person-to-person contact. Contrary to popular belief, dogs, cats, and other pets do not play a role in the transmission of human lice.

To cure a head-lice infestation, crush blue stone (available at the drugstore) and mix it with homemade lard to form a paste. Part the hair several times and place a good amount of the paste in each part. Cover the head for several hours and then shampoo.

To cure red bug, or chigger, bites, rub bites or itchy places with salty pork skin or use kerosene oil and one tablespoon table salt. Household ammonia is also good.

Tapeworms

It was inconceivable for me to believe worms could be in your stomach. Aunt Dollie said it really happened, and I believed it. My initial thought was that the worm would come from eating an apple or other fruits or vegetables with worms in them. I could imagine them turning over and over as she explained this. We sat on the front porch, Aunt Dollie in her rocking chair and me on the wooden steps.

I wanted to know where the worms lived and how big they were. She said you could have more than one. We sat in the evening sun as she shared a vivid explanation of how worms were said to get in your stomach. Some children would eat dirt, and worms could be imbedded in the dirt. Also, walking barefoot where dogs or animals lay and released waste was thought to be a culprit of the infestation. How could a worm go through the bottom of your foot and end up in your stomach? Her explanation was if you had a cut on the bottom of your foot, they could enter through the opening and work their way to the large intestine that led to your stomach. Eating too many sweets was also thought to cause an infestation.

She recalled that my grandmother would not allow them to eat too many green apples from the tree, and they were made to rinse all fruits from the vine. The meat from the smokehouse had to be fully cured before anyone was allowed to consume it. I began to wonder if I could have worms in my stomach. I felt my stomach and looked at it. Aunt Dollie thought that was so funny, but she stopped short to tell me that worms could not be detected in the stomach without an X-ray. My next question was how they could see in your stomach.

Children would show symptoms of what she called a wormy stomach. If they did not eat and complained of a stomachache, or if they curled up in a fetal position and whined when they were sleeping, older people would suspect the child had worms. I then wanted to know what happened when a child was suspected to have worms in his or her stomach. Well, she said, they would have to drink salt water and try to have a bowel movement or eat golden seal roots. Sometimes children's stomachs would be so upset that they would gag, heave, and throw up.

"I never had worms, but your cousins did," she said. I could imagine them turning over and over from the discomfort as she explained further. I ran away when she told me she saw my great-aunt across the field with a jar of the worms. Although I ran away, I came back because I wanted to hear the end of the story. She continued, "Aunt Ruby had a molasses jar with water and four worms my cousin Ben had passed."

"What in the world do you mean when you say he 'passed' them?" I asked. She explained that the worms had come from his feces, and my aunt took the worms from his waste, washed them off, and brought them to show my grandmother and the neighbors how long and wide they were. Aunt Dollie described them as flat and white with little lines on them. I did not want to hear anymore.

If you do have tapeworm infestation, chances are that you won't even be aware of it. Even if you do experience symptoms, they will hardly be noticeable and will most probably be misdiagnosed, being attributed to common ailments such as upset stomach, irritable bowel syndrome, or even stress. As a matter of fact, most people only notice they have a tapeworm when they see the bodies of the headless worm in their stool.

When you read through this list of symptoms, it will become clear why the symptoms of tapeworm infestation are so commonly misdiagnosed. Hence, you will have to be your best advocate to make the correct diagnosis and treatment. Some of the signs of infection are constipation, diarrhea, discomfort in the abdomen, and segments of tapeworm in the feces or clothes. Weakness caused due to poor absorption of nutrients into the body, loss of appetite, and weight loss are also symptoms of intestinal infection. If the infection has moved out of the intestine and infected other tissues by forming cysts, serious problems can ensue.

Neurologic symptoms such as seizures may be observed. Cystic masses, bacterial infection, and allergic reactions are among the serious symptoms of tapeworm infection in humans. If you or your doctor suspect that you have a tapeworm infection, an antibody test will be able to diagnose the infection. If there are neurologic symptoms, an MRI can be used to locate the cysts. Tapeworm infection is usually cured in most people. Some infections may last a long time, though, depending on the affected organ.

To cure tapeworm infestation, give a drop of turpentine the first night, two drops the second night, and so on as to your age. This can be given on a spoon of sugar. When the turpentine has been given, boil a tablespoonful of castor oil the next morning and take one tablespoon. Be sure to rub the navel with turpentine each night, especially after taking the oil; rub around the navel area for stomach or pin worms. If you fail to rub the stomach, they will knot up around the navel and remain in the stomach.

175 Years of Home Remedies

Aunt Dollie collected homemade remedies from her senior citizen friends, family members, and neighbors. I have some of her manuscripts in cookbooks and kitchen drawers. These remedies are obviously brown and tattered from aging; however, I can yet read them. Aunt Dollie often reminisced about sitting and assisting with sick relatives and friends, and if they passed away, she said, "We would stay with the body all night and talk about their life. Sometimes the doctors did not know as much as we knew about helping the sick; we learned how to use nature and what God made to cure the ills and ailments we had."

She gazed around with an expression of pride, sighed, and said, "Mama knew how to take care of you and she was a caregiver to Daddy and us children." We sat at her metal table eating roasted pecans and talked about her memories of yesterday. It was fall, and the air was crisp and cool; the trees and grass displayed the impeccable images of fall colors. I could imagine our Choctaw ancestors harvesting the garden vegetables and preparing the cured meat for the winter they would encounter.

I could not conceive how a family could survive without some modern conveniences. How did they sleep, bathe, cook, clean, and do things that had to be done for everyday living? I was actually sitting there talking and looking at the person who lived during that time and survived. Aunt Dollie and I sat there crunching the buttery roasted pecans, and between each crunch I asked questions and waited for a response. Did they use leaves or tree bark for medical antibiotics? How were children vaccinated? How were people quarantined from infectious diseases? What was used if babies could not drink the mother's milk? How did they survive? When homemakers cooked, did they consider salty, fatty, high-cholesterol ingredients? My family was very clean; however, did they have fresh clean food and water? How were dishes washed? How did their body stay clean after working very long hours in unhealthy conditions? Aunt Dollie's response to all of my questions was simply, "We did what we had to do and made do with what we had."

I perceived from her facial expression and body language that she was not at ease with the conversation; her voice lagging, she spoke softly. "You know, I do not remember our family wanting for anything. We had plenty, and Mama always shared what we had with others. We did not get sick much; we played and worked so hard no germs or diseases could stick to us. If we did come down with something, Mama always knew how to mix something up that made us feel better."

Hint: A little bit of asafetida tied in a soft cloth around the neck will keep diseases away.

Our conversations gave me the impression that they never were hungry or malnourished. Aunt Dollie told me how they made soda water. She said, "We had soda water to drink sometimes; the girls would make it right at the kitchen table." It was fascinating to learn how they would make their own soft drinks! The drinks were sweet, made from sugar, and the flavor was added from the juice of citrus fruits such as lemons, oranges, and limes. She explained how they made the soft drinks. "We took a bucket and added lemon juice, sugar, and baking soda; then we would cover the bucket and let the mixture fizz up and stand for a while. Afterward we would add water and have us some soda water."

Pellagra

I had never heard of "pellagra"; however, Aunt Dollie told me all about it. This was a condition of being malnourished, a diet with a lack of necessary nutrients. When I returned home, I read more about this condition in the encyclopedia. I understood this condition happened when the body lacked niacin, which could be consumed by eating fish, meat, and eggs. I was really surprised when the information stated Native Americans with a diet mostly of corn developed pellagra. This could be the reason why people shared what they had with one another, especially meat. Knowing my Choctaw ancestors grew and ate a lot of corn, it concerned me if Aunt Dollie knew of someone in our family with this condition, considering she did not dwell on the subject.

This cure for pellagra was found in Aunt Dollie's collection. I laughed about this cure, until Aunt Dollie informed me this really was a cure.

Time has changed so many things, but my dear mother had pellagra and this remedy really cured her. Doctors gave her only two months to live. She was told by an elderly neighbor to get her husband to go to the woods and find a bush of yellow root, dig it up, wash it well, put it in water, and bring it to a boil. When the mixture turned dark yellow, she was to drink a cup three times a day. For quite a long time, she left it sitting on the stove. Every time she cooked, she would move that pan over and bring the mixture to a good boil. Following these instructions, she was cured.

Asthma

Burn rabbit tobacco and let the asthmatic person inhale the fumes. It will help with breathing. Drinking a glass of warm milk before going to bed is recommended to help the person sleep.

Sitting under summer leaves will cure asthma and hay fever.

Gather ginseng leaves. Dry and beat them into a powder. Put the powder in a pan, place a hot coal on top, and inhale the smoke.

Keep a Chihuahua around the house.

Drinking a tea made from sumac leaves is a good cure for any kind of asthma and hay fever.

Wild plum bark tea is also good for asthma.

Coughs

To make cough syrup, put three or four pieces of peppermint candy and one teaspoon of paregoric in a small bottle. Fill it with whiskey. Take as needed for a cough.

Boil one lemon slowly in water for ten minutes. Cut the lemon and extract the juice. Put the juice in a regular drinking glass. Add one ounce of glycerin. Fill the glass with honey and stir before taking one teaspoon.

Melt two tablespoons of butter. Add one tablespoon of apple cider vinegar, one tablespoon of sugar, a pinch of salt, and a dash of pepper. Take one teaspoonful to relieve coughs.

Saturate brown sugar with whiskey. Take only as needed for a cough.

To make a larger portion of a cough remedy, use one-half cup honey, three teaspoons paregoric, and one-half cup whiskey.

Mix dry mustard with water and a bit of flour; spread over a cloth. Oil the chest and lay the mustard plaster cloth on the chest. Keep watch that it does not blister.

Coughs and Sore Throats

Take one teaspoon sugar mixed with a few drops of kerosene oil.

Mix one cup honey with one-third cup whiskey. Take one teaspoon every few hours for relief.

Make a cough syrup by boiling some cherry bark, honey, and a bit of whiskey until it thickens. Take a teaspoon as needed for a cough.

To make a good cough syrup, carefully mix one-third cup honey, one-third cup whiskey, and one-third cup lemon juice. Take one spoonful at a time.

Another remedy given that was found to be good for the throat and colds is a combination of whiskey and rock candy. This was also really good for the flu.

Croup

Melt butter and add sugar and vinegar. Take one teaspoon.

Roast onions and drink their juice.

Laryngitis

Use equal amounts of tallow, turpentine, and Vicks VapoRub. Heat, put on a cloth, and apply to the chest. Be sure to wash this off and use talcum powder before going out in the cold the next day.

Tonsillitis

Make a tea from catnip leaves. Wet a cloth with this, and put it around the throat.

Breathe moist, steamy air made from water and Vicks VapoRub for at least thirty minutes three to four times a day.

Colds and Congestion

For back and muscle pains caused by flu, take a few drops of turpentine on a teaspoon of sugar at bedtime.

On a piece of flannel cloth, spread Vicks VapoRub, turpentine, and tar. Heat and place on the chest to relieve congestion. Do not wear during the daylight; use only when going to bed.

Make a plaster of boiled onions and place on the chest to relieve congestion.

Sore Throat

Wear a dirty sock around the neck when going to bed.

Combine pine boughs and water in a container and heat. As steam appears, place a towel over the head and inhale or gulp the steam. It's good for sore throats and laryngitis.

Eat lemons to clear up sore throats and help relieve coughs.

Soak a cured tobacco leaf in vinegar. Wrap it around your neck. Secure with a long cotton stocking.

Gargle one teaspoon baking soda and two aspirins mixed in a large glass of water two or three times a day.

Open your mouth and allow someone to blow sulfur through a reed on a sore throat.

Diverticulitis

Diverticulitis occurs when the lining of the large intestine is inflamed, causing severe abdominal pain.

After each meal, take a teaspoonful of petroleum jelly. If you feel you cannot take it that often, be sure to take it at night. It will fill the little pockets in the intestines so the food cannot get in and cause infections.

To swallow it easily, take a small swallow of blackberry or concord wine. Next, take a heaping teaspoon of petroleum jelly and a large swallow of wine. The petroleum jelly will roll up like a marble and go right down. Otherwise, it will stick in your throat and teeth; you probably would never try it again. If you will follow this treatment, you may eat anything you want without having any more trouble. When you do get careless with this treatment, trouble begins.

Bleeding

Use a mixture of soot from the chimney and lard or oil. Place a spiderweb across the wound. If the cut is small, wet a cigarette paper and place it over the cut. Bleeding can be stopped by pouring acid iron mineral (available at the drugstore) on the cut. Regardless of how bad the wound is, keep pouring. It will turn black and cake the wound until you can get to the doctor. Every person needs a bottle.

If you cut your finger or hand, cover it generously with black pepper (it will not burn). It stops bleeding, promotes healing, and helps with soreness.

Wet a tea bag and place it on the bleeding spot.

The Eyes

If a particle, grit, or anything else gets in your eye, put a flaxseed in the eye and keep the eye shut. It will work the foreign object out.

For a welders' eye burn, scrape an Irish potato and place the scraping over the eye while lying down.

Take two crushed aspirins and apply them with ice over the eye. Take two aspirins orally and relax.

If eyes are red and irritated, one drop of castor oil in the eye relieves irritation.

For soreness or irritation, combine one pint water with one teaspoon of salt (not iodized). Keep in a handy place. Irrigate the eyes several times a day and night. Sniffing this solution into the nostrils and gargling will relieve a sore or scratchy throat.

Earache

A few drops of oil heated to lukewarm will relieve an earache. Two or three drops of warm paregoric in the ear or two or three drops of warm sweet oil will sooth the earache.

Note that it is important to know how warm a medication should be to pour in the ear. Heat it in a spoon; hold the spoon to the side of your face and turn the spoon sideways so you can barely feel the oil when it touches your face. Never pour oil in the ear that is too cold or too hot.

Stomach Spasms

Slowly eat a dry boiled ham sandwich with a cup of hot tea. Another person says a glass of warm milk and a slice of white bread will do the same. Go out and dig some golden seal roots—they are good for stomach troubles.

Hiccups

If you have the hiccups, hold your breath and count to ten.

If you see someone with hiccups, scare them, and the hiccups will stop.

When you have the hiccups, drink something hot and real sweet.

For hiccups, eat two teaspoons of damson preserves. If they do not stop, repeat after a few minutes. Only in rare cases is a third dose needed. (Eat the preserves without bread.)

Scalp

Warm vinegar applied to the scalp will remove dandruff.

For an itchy scalp, beat two or three raw eggs. Wet the hair with warm water and rub in the beaten eggs with the tips of your fingers. Rinse hair thoroughly with lukewarm water. Brush thoroughly while hair is drying.

Don't cut your hair in the dark of the moon, or it will cause baldness.

Boils

Take a wasp nest, make a paste by mixing it with water, and put it on a boil to bring it to a head.

Take a piece of fat meat and put it on a boil to help to bring it to a head. Cover with gauze.

Eat such things as sorghum molasses, raisins, and onions to help this ailment.

Take Octagon Laundry Soap (a small amount) and mix it with sugar. Make a salve, and apply it to the boil. Use a piece of fat meat on the boil, and tie a rag over it to hold it in place. Scrape an Irish potato and rotate it. This will draw the fever out and bring the boil to a head.

Warts

Mix one tablespoon baking soda in two teaspoons water. Rub it on the wart several times daily.

Rub castor oil on the wart each night and morning, rubbing it gently twenty times or so to work into the wart until it disappears.

Rub the wart with a piece of garlic every day.

Stump water is real good for warts and other skin ailments.

Steal someone's dishrag, rub it on the warts, and hide it. The warts will go away.

Make the wart bleed. Put a drop of blood on a kernel of corn and feed it to the rooster.

Another way to take off warts is to put iodine on them several nights in a row. They will soon go away.

Headache

For a mild headache, wet a towel in cold water and hold it on the forehead. You can also use an ice pack on the head.

Wet a piece of brown paper bag with vinegar and coat it with baking soda. Tie it on the head with something tight.

Bind wilted beet leaves on the forehead.

Mix a little turpentine and beef tallow in a bandage and tie it tightly around the head.

Fish Bone Stuck in the Throat

Eat cornbread. The bone will disappear.

Eat a lemon or part of one. The lemon juice causes the bone to dissolve.

Eat a banana to help move the bone.

Heartburn

Mix one teaspoon baking soda in a half glass of water. After about half an hour, if symptoms are relieved, take a cup of warm milk to keep down acid rebound.

Monthly Period Pain

Those who suffer pain and discomfort should try ginger tea. Place one-half teaspoon of ginger in a cup and pour one cup of boiling water over it. Sweeten to taste, and add one to two tablespoons whiskey. Drink it, and lie down for a while.

Sunburn

Mix baking soda and vinegar to make a paste. Put it on the area overnight.

Strong tea applied on the sunburn will instantly take the fire out.

Nosebleed

Stop a nosebleed by wetting a piece of brown paper or paper towel in cold water and placing it under the lip. Hold the head back.

Pack nostrils with cotton dipped in lemon juice; leave for some time to let the blood clot. (This always worked for severe nosebleeds.)

Leg Ache

Tie a string soaked in turpentine around your leg and then rub the leg in kerosene. This eases the pain every time.

Chapped Skin

Apple cider vinegar applied several times a day will restore natural acidity to skin. At night, rub with vegetable oil for chapped hands.

Vaseline is good for chapped hands and lips.

Upset Stomach

For upset stomach, colitis, and diarrhea, drink a cup of hot tea.

Diarrhea

Boil and drink yellow root.

A tea of red oak bark is also good for diarrhea.

Make a tea of wild peppermint and drink.

Measles

Give a measles patient a hot drink to make him or her break out. Others say to give a cold drink. Try one—if it doesn't work on your patient, try the other.

Bruises

Apply an ice pack or a cloth dipped in ice water and wrung out to a bruise.

Insect Stings

Apply chewing tobacco juice to the sting.

Use household ammonia on an insect sting.

Apply a paste of baking soda and table vinegar.

Swelling and Sprain

Use a vinegar and clay poultice. It works well to reduce the swelling and soreness from a sprain.

Make a paste of dirt dabber nest and vinegar. Apply to the affected area and wrap loosely with gauze.

Bronchitis

Spread pine tar on a cloth, fold the cloth, and grease on the side next to the skin. Change the plaster once or twice a week.

Springtime Tonic

Boil together some sage and water until it is the color of dark tea. Refrigerate it and take it three times a day as a tonic.

Thicken sulfur and molasses until it makes a thick paste. Take a tablespoonful of paste for three days, skip two days, and then take one tablespoonful for one day. This was a must for survival in olden days.

Pains

Heat table salt in a heavy cast-iron skillet. When hot, put it in a cloth bag and apply it to the painful area. Relief comes more quickly than an electric heating pad.

Lullaby Pill

Mix one cup honey and three tablespoons vinegar. Mix well, and take two teaspoons at bedtime for sleep.

Itch

Use homemade lard thickened with sulfur and a few drops of whiskey. Mix until it is the consistency of an ointment. Spread it over the entire body for several hours. Burn all used clothes, and put on clean ones.

Sores

Hold a piece of lightwood over a fire to get the pine rosin. Mix it with sulfur, and apply the mix to heal a sore.

Painkiller

Roast some poke roots by the fire. Scrape them clean with a knife and grind them up. Make a poultice out of the powder and apply it to the bottom of the feet. This will draw the pain out of anywhere in the body.

Sores, Boils, Carbuncle, and Staph Infection

Trim bark from limbs of an alder tag bush (found in marshland or around a creek). Mix it with water, and boil it until you have a brown-colored tea. Refrigerate. Drink a glassful of tea in the morning and at night until infection disappears. A sure cure!

Sore with Fever and Infection

Crumble some homemade biscuits and add enough sweet milk to make a soft poultice. Cover the sore area as you would with a salve. Cover with gauze and then wrap in plastic to hold moisture. Sometimes the fever is so hot that it almost cooks the poultice into a pancake.

Bee Sting or Stepping on a Rusted Nail

Boil peach-tree leaves for thirty to forty minutes. Drain the water, add one teaspoon of salt, and thicken with cornmeal. Make a poultice and put it on the infected area. Leave on overnight to remove fever and swelling. Real good!

Snake Bites

Keep the victim quiet and reassure him or her. Transport him or her to a source of medical help as soon as possible. Immobilize the arm or leg in a position below the heart. Apply constricting bands for the arms or legs two to four inches above the bite. You should be able to place your finger under the band when it is in place. Make half-inch incisions (not crosscut) through the skin at each fang mark and over the venom deposit. The incisions should be only through the skin and in the long axis of the limb, not across. Do not cut into nerves or muscles. Apply suction with the kit or mouth for thirty to sixty minutes. Venom will not poison your stomach, but try not to swallow. Rinse your mouth. Wash cuts thoroughly with soap and water and blot dry. Apply sterile dry dressing. Treat for shock and give artificial respiration, if necessary. Call ahead to the hospital for antivenom.

Moles That Bear Watching

Moles on your ankles or feet

Moles that become irritated from the rubbing of clothing or underarm clothing

Moles that change size, shape, or color

Brown Spots on Hands and Face

Castor oil was rubbed on spots every night until they disappeared.

Buttermilk was applied to spots several times a day.

Equal parts cucumber juice and lemon juice applied daily.

To Harden Soft Nails

Soak in warm olive oil twice a week.

Foot Perspiration and Odor

Mix one cup talcum powder with cornstarch. Add a teaspoon of salicylic acid, and dust your feet really well.

Rub some mutton (meat of a fully grown sheep) on the bottom of your feet and hold them to a fire.

One-Step Home Remedies

A buckeye carried in the pocket will cure rheumatism.

A piece of nutmeg tied around the neck will prevent neuralgia.

Tatter (cradle cap)—rub a green persimmon across the affected area of the head.

Drink blackberry wine for an upset stomach.

Stir molasses in water and drink for energy.

Drink sienna tea or black draught as a laxative.

Rub kerosene oil around the ankle for red bugs.

Eat cooked onions with sugar for help with croup.

For a gash or cut from stepping on a nail, pour kerosene oil on the area.

For a chest cold, rub camphorated oil on the chest.

To calm a colic baby, try simethicone drops.

To drain the gallbladder, drink water with Epsom salt.

For rheumatism, drink one cup of hot water with lemon juice before breakfast.

For liver ailment, drink dandelion root and May apples tea.

Wear a dirty sock around the neck when going to bed for a sore throat.

Soak tired, aching feet in warm salt water.

Press a small wad of cotton under the corner of an ingrown toenail and leave for several days.

For frostbite, immerse hands or feet in cold water and alternate taking out of water and putting back in water.

Apply aloe plant juice to a burn. To ease the pain of a burn and prevent blistering, grab a bottle of vanilla flavor and dab some on the affected area. Use a fire plant on a burn, or rub a burn with butter.

Run cold water over a burn. It will take the fire out.

Make a paste of baking soda and water and apply to itchy skin.

Night sweats can be cured by setting a pan of cold water under your bed.

For cuts, wash the cut with warm, soapy water; apply milk antiseptic. Then dress with a thin layer of petroleum jelly and bandage.

If you get a sunburn that threatens discomfort, soak in a tub full of cool water with a cup full of baking soda. Do not use a washcloth.

Century-Old Household and Garden Tips

Don't plant cucumbers or beans when the plant is blossoming or they will bloom too much.

To remove mildew, pretreat the stain with detergent and launder. If stain remains, sponge with hydrogen peroxide. Rinse and launder using bleach safe for the fabric.

On cold days when the fire in the fireplace sputters and cracks, the fire is calling for snow, and it will snow within three days.

Never use a tree for firewood that has been struck by lightning.

Asafetida worn around the neck in the winter will keep away disease (probably because the smell is so strong that no germs will come near it).

Chill cheese to grate it more easily.

To remove tar and asphalt, act before the stain is dry. Pour fireproof engine oil through the cloth and repeat.

Dip a spoon in hot water to measure shortening or butter. The fat will slip out more easily.

A clean clothespin provides a cool handle to steady the cake tin when removing a hot cake.

The sex of a chicken can be foretold by the visitors on Easter Day. If the majority of the guests are men, most of the chickens will be roosters, but if there are more women, then you can look for a pullet flock.

A leaf of lettuce dropped into the pot absorbs the grease from the top of soup. The leaf serves no purpose, so throw it away.

Try using a thread instead of a knife to cut a warm cake.

Use the divider from an ice tray to cut biscuits in a hurry. Shape dough to conform to the size of the divider and cut. After baking, biscuits will separate at the dividing lines.

To remove chewing gum, harden gum by rubbing it with ice. Scrape as much as possible without damaging the fabric. Sponge it with fireproof engine rinse and launder.

Use a can opener with a smooth edge and remove both ends from a flat can (the size in which tuna is usually packed), and you will have a perfect mold for poaching eggs.

If you keep a mule shoe in the oven, it will keep hawks from getting the chickens.

If you have a leaky water faucet, every two seconds you are wasting fifty-four gallons of water.

Colored gloves that no longer suit your wardrobe can be dyed a basic brown or black.

To remove ballpoint ink from clothes, sponge the stain with acetone or amyl acetate.

Make your own placemats in any size and shape by cutting oil cloth shapes with pinking shears.

To clean a dirty iron, use a damp paper towel and a little bit of toothpaste. Then wipe it clean with another damp paper towel. Make sure the iron is cool.

To make your iron smooth, rub it on waxed paper.

You can remove white water marks on tabletops and other furniture by applying mayonnaise on spot and rubbing it in. Let it stand for an hour or more, and wipe it clean with a soft cloth.

Add one grated raw potato with each pound of ground beef for juicy hamburgers.

Thaw frozen meat by putting it in a dishwasher or washing machine and turning it on for a few minutes.

You can thaw frozen meat in an egg carton, and then all the water will be in the carton. You can simply throw it away.

If you need a right-handed glove and only have a left one, just turn it inside out.

To keep rubber gloves from sticking together, put the bottom of a tin can in the glove. The air can go into the glove, and it will not stick together.

If there should be a small hole in finger of a rubber glove, turn the glove inside out and put tape on the hole and turn it back to the right side.

To make an iron slick so it will iron smoothly and easily, occasionally rub beeswax on it when ironing.

Glazing with ice is one method to protect fish during storage.

Butter and cheese may be kept six to twelve months when wrapped in vapor-proof paper.

Cream can be frozen in glass jars and kept for six months.

Freeze eggs by separating yolks from whites. For yolks, add two tablespoons of sugar or one teaspoon of salt for each yolk.

Do not keep frozen food too long; keep a record of food stored.

A vegetable brush is just the thing to remove scum from jelly or soup.

A little lime kept on shelves where jelly and preserves are stored will prevent the formation of mold.

To clean jar lids, put lids in a pan and cover with sweet milk. Let stand until clabbered. Take out and wash and they will be like new.

Jam or jelly that is hard or sugary will be freshened if you leave it in a warm oven until the sugar softens.

Never leave grease melting on the stove.

Try a little cream of tartar in your seven-minute icing. It will not get dry and crack.

Never leave an electric iron on when leaving the room.

Put baked apples or stuffed peppers in muffin tins; the fruits and vegetables will hold their shape.

Use leftover wallpaper to decorate some of the accessories in the same room. It is also good to line dresser drawers.

Dip the ends of cord or rope in shellac to prevent them from fraying.

Nylon cords should be burned on the end to keep them intact.

Rub a candle over the address label of a package for mailing. The wax will weatherproof the label.

Cover instructions with clear plastic tape on bottles and jars.

Do not beat egg whites in aluminum; eggs darken aluminum.

To keep a black iron frying pan from sticking, wash it while hot in cold water. Dry and store.

Tape fingers with first aid tape before grating or chopping with a sharp knife.

When using paraffin for sealing jelly, place it in a coffee can to melt. Use what is needed and store the remainder in the same can until you need to use more.

Dip a raw potato into scouring powder to scrub the corners of rusted cake and pie pans.

Place dressing for fresh fruit salad into a bowl first; then drop each piece of fruit as it is cut into the bowl. This gives it less of a chance to darken.

To keep a cake fresh longer, cut the cake in half and cut a slice from each half. Push the two halves together and the cake does not dry out on the cut side.

As we grow older and wiser, we should talk less and say more.

A good laugh is sunshine in a house.

A clean mouth and an honest hand will take a man through any land.

Many do come to bring their clothes to church rather than themselves.

Brush milk or cream on top of two crust pies for a nice brown pie.

Shortly before taking cupcakes from the oven, place a large marshmallow on each for the frosting.

Wish not so much to live long as to live well.

Get your happiness out of your work, or you will never know what real happiness is.

Tomorrow is the greatest laborsaving device ever thought of.

The gifts of things are never as precious as the gift of thought.

On your stove, cover drip pans with foil under each surface unit.

An extra snack a day can add as much as ten pounds in one year.

Wash items to be ironed first. You can do the ironing while other loads wash and dry.

Read the label first. Some clothing must be washed before worn.

Perk up sweet pickle relish with chili sauce, mustard, or Worcestershire sauce.

Keep time-saving appliances and frequently used utensils within easy reach to make meal preparation easier.

Don't throw out dried-out cheese. Grate it and store it in covered container with paper towels. When frozen, stack and store in plastic bags. Reheat in the stove.

To ease a tight ring on a finger, coat the ring with petroleum jelly.

Petroleum jelly is a good lubricant and moisturizer.

Before storing ice skates or roller skates, protect the binding, blades, and metal edges with petroleum jelly.

Speed the action on can openers and other appliances, but only if operating instructions call for lubrication.

For a variety of soups, freeze either chicken or beef broth. When ready for soup, add vegetables or noodles.

Attach four snap clothespins to the edge of a cake pan. When the cake rises above the four legs and you turn your cake pan upside down, it is adequate.

To retard corrosion, coat the metal surface of garden tools with oil.

When cream will not whip, add an egg white to your cream. Chill it and it will whip.

Do not leave a spoon or other metal in a pot that you want to come to a boil quickly. The metal deflects the heat.

To prevent a vegetable salad from becoming sodden when it stands for a few hours, place a saucer upside down on the bottom of the bowl before filling it with salad. The moisture will run underneath and the salad will remain fresh and crisp.

Food in the refrigerator should be covered; cold dry air evaporates the moisture from food and deposits it as frost on the evaporator coils.

To protect the motor of a refrigerator, plug it into a separate electrical outlet on an individual circuit.

Wet ink stains may be removed by washing the stained item in buttermilk.

Equal parts of table salt and cream of tartar will remove rust stains. Wet the spots and spread the mixture on thickly; place the material in the sun.

Soften axle grease or tar stains with lard and then soak in turpentine. Use a knife to carefully scrape off all the loose surface dirt. Sponge clean with turpentine and rub gently until dry.

Always allow plenty of space around the refrigerator for free air circulation so the condenser coils will be properly cooled.

When you fry country-style steak, slightly salt and then flour the steak. Let stand ten to fifteen minutes. The batter will stay on better while cooking.

When you fry fish, spread newspapers in front of the stove. The grease spatters will fall on the newspaper. When finished, roll up the paper and discard. It is easier than scrubbing the floor.

A little buttermilk on baked potatoes is as good as sour cream.

When cutting marshmallows or dates, dip scissors into water first.

Pour a little vanilla on a piece of cotton and place it in the refrigerator to eliminate odors.

To prevent mildew on refrigerator gaskets and inside, wipe them with pure vinegar. The acid will kill the mildew fungus.

Plain rubbing alcohol will remove fly specks when applied with a facial tissue. This is excellent for cleaning your eyeglasses.

Put a dab of peanut butter on gum stuck in hair and rub gently between your fingers. The peanut butter will loosen chewing gum.

If you scorch an article while ironing, just wet the goods, apply cornstarch to the spot, and rub well.

Camphor will remove fruit stains from table linens if it is applied before the cloth is wet.

To remove coffee or tea stains, soak the cloth overnight in a large pan of strong vinegar water and hang it dripping wet in the sun. Better yet, put it directly on green grass.

Scratched mahogany woodwork can be repaired by painting it with iodine. After applying iodine, go over the entire surface with furniture polish.

Clean costume jewelry by putting the jewelry in a bowl and pouring rubbing alcohol over it. Let it set a few minutes and then wipe.

Line drawers with plastic placemats for a clean, flat surface.

Plastic bags may be used to store out-of-season shoes.

Cut a plastic bleach jug in half. The top can be used as a funnel with a handle. The bottom can be used to clean paintbrushes.

To quickly and smoothly remove the skins of fruits, let them sit in boiling water for a few minutes before peeling.

Planting Time

What people call the dark night (dark of the moon) is the time from full moon to the new moon, or the shrinking of the moon. The other half of the phase from the new moon to the full is known as the light of the moon.

Plants that grow underground, such as potatoes, turnips, onions, and so forth, must be planted in the dark of the moon. For instance, okra all will go to tops. Beans, peas, tomatoes, and such that have their crop above the ground should be planted in the light of the moon. Potatoes should be harvested in the light of the moon, or they will rot.

In the southern region, beans should not be planted until after the first whippoorwill hollers and the beans should be planted in the morning, not evening. The best planting time for lettuce is about February 14. Cucumbers planted should be planted about May 1, watermelons about May 10, and turnips should be harvested July 25.

Always avoid the first day of the new moon for planting. Also avoid the days on which the moon changes quarters.

If you dig a hole in the ground to plant something, you will never have enough dirt to refill the hole if it is the shrinking of the moon.

When cooking during the shrinking of the moon, watch your pot boil. You will have a hard time keeping enough water in the pot, and your food will burn.

Pick your apples and pears during the old moon, and the bruised spots will dry up. If picked in the new moon, the spots will rot.

Plant sunflowers with your pole beans. This saves time spent in cutting poles and also protects beans from frost.

Plant radishes and cucumbers together to keep bugs off the cucumbers.

When sowing carrot seeds, mix them with radish seed. Then pull the radishes and leave the carrots to grow in their place.

To prevent rust on garden tools, keep a thick rag soaked in kerosene handy for wiping off the tools when you come in from the garden.

Plant parsley in small pots on your windowsill. These pots of green keep spring in your kitchen all winter and will be an ever-ready garnish for meats. You can sell the surplus at your church bazaar.

When planting peas in the spring, plant zinnias in the same row at the same time. Your flowers will bloom long after the peas are gone. This saves space and beautifies your garden at the same time.

When you plant turnip greens, mustard greens, and the like, be sure to plant plenty of radishes to keep the lice out of your garden.

Grow radishes in turnip greens and chives and marigolds in gardens as repellants. The strong odors of herbs serve as good insect control.

Lime and wood ashes mixed together can be sprinkled on squash for bugs, snails, and such.

Wood ashes control caterpillars and worms.

Tar water weakens potato bugs and beetles.

Sprays made from marigolds, chrysanthemums, and radishes (tea) are repellants for worms and insects.

In the Kitchen

To keep cakes from sticking, sprinkle the tins with equal parts of flour and fine sugar.

When bread is baking, a small dish of water in the oven will help to keep the crust from getting too hard.

When separating the yolk from the white of an egg, if you drop a part of the egg yolk into the white, moisten a cloth with cold water and touch it to the yolk. It will adhere to the cloth.

If you heat lemons well before using, there will be twice the quantity of juice.

When cooking cauliflower, add lemon juice or vinegar to keep it snowy white.

If an egg cracks on one end, crack the other end and you can boil it without the contents coming out of the shell.

Wash Day

One tablespoon black pepper added to the first suds in which you are washing cottons will keep the color from running.

Dampened clothes will not mildew for several days if you put them into the lower part of the refrigerator.

When you are washing and rinsing colored material, one teaspoon Epsom salt added to each gallon of water will prevent even the most delicate shades from fading or running.

When washing or ironing, put a thick rug under your feet and you will not tire so easily.

Tablecloths and sheets should be folded crosswise occasionally. It will make them last longer.

To remove iron mold ink from materials, steep the material in a hot solution of salt or lemon, one tablespoon of salt to one quart boiling water, or simply place the stained part over a basin. Cover the stains with salt and pour the boiling water through. Repeat if necessary.

Grease spots generally may be removed with hot water and soap. If stains have become fixed by long standing, they may be removed by chloroform or naphtha. If any of these chemicals are used, keep them at a safe distance from fire or artificial light.

Soften axle grease or tar stains with lard and then soak in turpentine. Use a knife to carefully scrape off all the loose surface dirt. Sponge clean with turpentine and rub gently until dry.

Equal parts of table salt and cream of tartar will remove rust stains. Wet the spot and spread the mixture on thickly and then place the material in the sun.

To remove chewing gum from fabrics, rub with ice. The gum will roll off and leave no marks.

Household Aids

Red ants can be kept out of the pantry if a small quantity of green sage is placed on the shelves.

To brighten tarnished silverware, let it soak for one hour in the water left after boiling white potatoes. It will come out bright as new.

A piece of bread crust inserted between the teeth when peeling an onion will stop the tears.

To clean silk from corn, brush with a hand scrub brush.

When putting a nail in a plastered wall, if it will not hold, fill the hole with steel wool; the nail will hold perfectly.

To remove discoloration from aluminum utensils, boil in a solution of water with a teaspoon of cream of tartar to one quart water for twenty minutes.

When boiling eggs, add a pinch of salt to the water to prevent cracking.

To remove nutmeats whole, pour boiling water over the nuts; let them stand all night before cracking.

To prevent grease from popping from the frying pan, sift about one-quarter teaspoon flour in it.

Make a solution of one tablespoon baking soda in two quarts of water for thirty minutes; remove stems and then make preserves or jam.

Add one ounce of cream cheese to your pastry mix when making a fruit pie; it makes it flaky and also gives a delightful flavor.

Save all juices from canned fruit when making salads. It is delicious in making gelatin desserts or sauces for puddings.

To remove milk rings, pour a little baking soda into the bottles. Add water, soak, and shake the bottle to hasten cleansing action. It sweetens while it cleans.

For easy cleaning of silver, put one teaspoon baking soda in each quart of water in an aluminum pan. Bring to a boil. Use enough water to cover the silver. Place silver in the solution for several minutes. Remove, rinse, and dry. The aluminum pan may be discolored in the process, so do not use one you care about.

Odors such as fish are quickly removed from pans by soaking them in baking soda water. Use two tablespoons of baking soda to each quart of water. Wash with soapy water, rinse, and dry.

Small grease fires may be extinguished by pouring baking soda over the burning area. Never throw water on a grease fire as it will cause it to spread.

To keep odors out of refrigerators, place an open box of baking soda inside the refrigerator. Change about every two months.

When baking a milk pudding, place the dish in a pan of water in the oven. This prevents the pudding from burning or boiling over.

Brush the bottom crust of a meat pie with an egg white to prevent the gravy from soaking in.

To keep cookies fresh and crisp in the jar, place crumpled tissue paper in the bottom.

To keep boiled syrup from crystallizing, add a pinch of baking soda.

Put cream or milk on top of two crust pies for nice brown pie spots.

Paint comes off windows if rubbed with a little nail polish remover.

Half ammonia and half water is a very good varnish remover.

If you rub petroleum jelly on your hands before starting a paint job, the paint washes off easily.

Pour one cup of bleach in a drain and let it set one hour. Then pour in boiling water to prevent the drain from stopping up.

To eliminate gas when eating pinto beans, put one tablespoon of castor oil to one quart of water.

Use potato flakes for thickening gravy instead of flour for lump-free gravy.

To remove the shell from hard-boiled eggs, crack the shell by tapping it gently all over. Roll the egg between your hands to loosen the shell. Peel the egg at the large end, holding it under running water or in a bowl of water.

Clean storm doors and windows by using a soft cloth dampened with gasoline.

Wrap good toilet soap in foil and put it under the couch to eliminate musty odors.

After cleaning silver, put two sticks of blackboard chalk in the chest with it.

Use lemon juice to clean stains in a bathtub.

To clean the rubber around a refrigerator door, use baking soda with water.

Sprinkle a frying pan with salt before meat is added, and the fat will not splatter.

Add one teaspoon lemon juice to each quart of water while you cook rice to make the grains stay separate and white.

To freshen up your vegetables—such as lettuce, spinach, and parsley—soak them in cold water to which a slice of lemon has been added.

When scalding milk, first rinse the pan in cold water to keep it from sticking.

When a recipe directs that eggs be slightly beaten, the eggs should be whipped only until the yolks and whites are just combined.

Use salad oil in molds for gelatin to come out easy.

Sprinkle cake plates with powdered sugar to keep cake from sticking to the serving plate.

Two and a half cups of raisins equals one pound.

Two cups of coarsely chopped nuts equals one pound.

When baking, always cream butter or margarine well before gradually adding sugar. Adding one to two tablespoons of water will make this mixture fluffier.

When baking a cake, add two tablespoons of boiling water to the butter and sugar mixture. This makes a finer texture.

To keep brown sugar from becoming hard, store it in a quart jar with the rubber seal and screw the cap on tight.

Cakes will come from pans without sticking if you place the pans on a damp cloth when you take them from the oven.

Cooked dried fruit or fig preserves make a substitute for dates.

To remove coffee or tea stains, moisten the material with glycerin and rub gently until the spot disappears.

When glass containers stick together, place the lower container in hot water and fill the upper container with cold water.

One cup of raw rice equals three cups of cooked rice.

When cooking eggs start with a cold pan to avoid sticking.

A thick layer of newspaper under a rug keeps the room warmer in the winter.

Sprinkle a little salt over the boilover in the oven, and it will stop the burning and take care of unpleasant odors.

To clean brass and copper, use a paste of one tablespoon each of flour, salt, and vinegar. Let it remain for an hour and then rub off with a soft cloth and wash. Use a soft brush for places that cannot be reached with a cloth.

Dry mix one cup baking soda, one cup salt, and one-quarter cup cream of tartar to clean drains. To use, put one-quarter cup into the drain and add one cup boiling water. When the bubbling stops, run water through the drain.

To clean darkened pans, fill them with water. Add two teaspoons cream of tartar. Simmer for ten minutes.

Leftover paint can be kept from drying out by pouring melted paraffin over the surface.

To make neglected paintbrushes pliable, place them in boiling vinegar to just cover and simmer for a few minutes. Wash in soap and warm water and dry.

Deep vases may be cleaned by allowing a solution of salt and vinegar to stand in them for a short time. Shake well, drain, and rinse with clean water.

A good bleach for stains on porcelain is peroxide with a few drops of household ammonia mixed with cream of tartar.

Mix one part white shoe polish and one part liquid floor polish. Polish your shoes, and this will clean your white shoes after you buff.

When bath towels wear in the middle, cut the ends into squares. Sew several pieces of tulle nylon netting to one side of each square. They make wonderful dishcloths.

To remove rust from a kitchen sink, add one-half teaspoon household ammonia to half a bottle of peroxide. Thoroughly soak a cloth with this liquid and sprinkle a generous amount of cream of tartar and scouring powder over the cloth. Work this into a paste and scrub the stained area. Allow as much paste as possible to remain on the stain. Rinse after an hour.

For exterior/interior painting, stir one teaspoon of vanilla extract into the paint. It will not change the color or texture of the paint; however, it will help you through the fresh paint odor in those first days.

To preserve the flavor of coffee after it has been ground, store it in the refrigerator.

For smoother iced drinks, a simple syrup of equal parts sugar and water boiled for ten minutes and kept in the refrigerator can be used as a sweetener.

Iced tea or coffee is greatly improved if the ice cubes are made of coffee or tea instead of water.

You can avoid cloudiness in iced tea by letting the freshly made tea cool slowly at room temperature.

When a recipe calls for sour milk and you have none, add one tablespoon vinegar to one cup sweet milk.

Add a small bit of dried orange peel to the teapot for a different-tasting tea.

When making bread crumbs from stale bread, place the slices on a board, cover them with a paper towel or paper bag, and roll them with a rolling pin.

Keep bread in the refrigerator in a closed container to keep it fresh.

Remove rust from a cement porch with a wire brush.

Store cornmeal in a closed container in the refrigerator to keep it fresh.

To prevent icing from running off a cake, dust a little cornstarch over the surface before icing.

To add a different taste to oatmeal cookies, add a small amount of grated orange peel to the batch.

Cover dried fruits and nuts with flour before adding them to cake batter. This will keep them from sinking to the bottom of the batter.

To prevent cupcakes in paper cups from burning on the bottom, turn a pan that fits the bottom of the muffin pan upside down under the pan in which the cupcakes are baked.

To keep meringue on a pie from being sticky when cut, while the meringue is hot, use a knife dipped in hot water to mark off the pieces of pie, cutting only through the meringue.

To keep egg yolks for several days in the refrigerator, cover them with cold water and put them in a covered container.

To eliminate the dark ring that separates the yolk from the whites of hard-boiled eggs, run cold water over the eggs immediately after cooking.

For a welcome change in fish, stuff it with rice and seasoning.

To select a tender chicken, make certain the flesh is firm and the breastbone is pliable and not broken.

To ripen green fruit, put it in a paper bag in a dark place for a few days.

It is easier to par pineapple if you slice it first.

To remove the skin of fruits quickly and smoothly, let them sit in boiling water a few minutes before peeling.

Canned pears filled with mint jelly make an attractive and delicious addition to a roast dinner.

Sausages can be parboiled or rolled in flour before frying to prevent them from bursting.

Ham will keep its juiciness if allowed to cool in the water it was cooked in.

To reheat leftover meat, heat it in the top of a double boiler to which a little gravy or water has been added.

To help tenderize tougher cuts of meats, cook tomatoes with it so the acid will help tenderize the meat.

Putting a toothpick through a clove of garlic before cooking will make the clove easy to find when the time comes to remove it.

Put herbs and spices in a piece of wet muslin for soup and stews.

If you use too much salt in the cooking of food, add a raw potato to it. This will absorb much of the salt.

Freshen wilted vegetables by soaking them in a basin of cold water to which the juice of a lemon or one tablespoon vinegar was added.

To draw out hidden insects inside heads of cabbage, collards, and cauliflower, let the vegetables stand for fifteen minutes in cold water containing a little salt or vinegar.

Cook carrots in their skins until tender, and the skins will easily slip off.

Place onions in boiling water for a few seconds to prevent your eyes from watering while cutting them.

Reheat baked potatoes by dipping them in hot water before warming them in a warm oven.

To keep old potatoes from darkening when they are boiling, add a small amount of milk to the cooking water.

To remove the odor of onion or garlic from a knife, run the blade through a potato.

When the top on a jar is hard to remove, let hot water run over the top of it to open it easily.

Use kitchen shears to chop small amounts of food.

The End

I extend my heartfelt thanks to my aunt Dollie Holmes Coleman (deceased) for sharing our family history, wisdom, home remedies, tips, and recipes—all of which she held dear to her heart.